K Nelson

I Am Canada

Heather Patterson

North Winds Press
An Imprint of Scholastic Canada Ltd.

For Finn — a bright piece of the Canadian mosaic
— H. P.

Photo Credits
Front cover: (above left and right) © First Light; (below left)
© Heiko Wittenborn; (below right) © First Light
Back cover: © First Light
Page 1: © Keith Douglas/First Light
Page 2: (left) © Quick Pixels; (right) © First Light
Page 3: (left) © First Light; (right) © iStockphoto
Page 4: © Design Pics Inc.
Page 5: © Design Pics Inc.
Page 6: (left) © First Light; (right) © Getty Images
Page 7: © First Light
Page 8: Courtesy of Michael Ptatschek
Page 9: © Peter Cade/Getty Images
Page 10: © Bernard Weil/Toronto Star
Page 11: Courtesy of Courtesy of Saskatchewan Industry and Resources
Page 12: © First Light
Page 13: © BananaStock Ltd.
Page 14: © First Light
Page 15: © First Light
Page 16: © iStockphoto

Page 17: (left) © First Light; (right) © Getty Images
Page 18: © BananaStock Ltd.
Page 19: © AbleStock
Page 20: (left) © Getty Images; (right) © Scholastic Canada Ltd.
Page 21: © Scholastic Canada Ltd.
Page 22: © Scholastic Canada Ltd.
Page 23: (left) © Scholastic Canada Ltd.; (right) © Catherine London
Page 24: (left) © World of Stock; (right) © Getty Images
Page 25: (left) Courtesy of Saskatchewan Industry and Resources; (right)
© First Light
Page 26: (left) © iStockphoto; (right) © Getty Images
Page 27: © iStockphoto
Page 28: (left) © First Light; (right) © Getty Images
Page 29: © iStockphoto
Page 30: © Rommel/Masterfile

Special thanks to Danielle H., Andrew, Serena and Danielle M.

Library and Archives Canada Cataloguing in Publication
Patterson, Heather, 1945-
I am Canada / Heather Patterson.

ISBN 0-439-95757-5

1. Canada--Pictorial works--Juvenile literature. 2. Canada--Juvenile
literature. I. Title.

FC58.P38 2006   j971'.0022'2   C2005-906603-2

6 5 4 3 2 1   Printed in Canada   06 07 08 09

I have space.

I read.

I learn.

I draw.

I dream.

I stay out late and see the northern lights.

I have time.

I watch.

I touch.

I listen.

I make up
my mind.

I decide to build a castle.

I am free.

I am Canada.

I am cool in summer and cozy in winter.

I am springy
in the spring

and floppy
in the fall.

I eat pizza
and perogies
and peppers.

I eat meatballs
and muffins
and mangoes.

I am quiet.

I am curious.

I am friendly.

I am funny.

I explain.

I explore.

I celebrate.

I am Canada.